ALPHA'S PUNISHMENT

AN ALPHA DOMS BONUS BOOK

ALPHA DOMS

RENEE ROSE

RENEE ROSE ROMANCE

Copyright © 2015-2024 Alpha's Punishment by Renee Rose. Originally published by Stormy Night Publications 2015

All rights reserved. This copy is intended for the original purchaser of this e-book ONLY. No part of this e-book may be reproduced, scanned, or distributed in any printed or electronic form without prior written permission from the author. Please do not participate in or encourage piracy of copyrighted materials in violation of the author's rights. Purchase only authorized editions.

Published in the United States of America

Renee Rose Romance

This e-book is a work of fiction. While reference might be made to actual historical events or existing locations, the names, characters, places and incidents are either the product of the author's imaginations or are used fictitiously, and any resemblance to actual persons, living or dead, business establishments, events, or locales is entirely coincidental.

This book contains descriptions of many BDSM and sexual practices, but this is a work of fiction and, as such, should not be used in any way as a guide. The author and publisher will not be responsible for any loss, harm, injury, or death resulting from use of the information contained within. In other words, don't try this at home, folks!

WANT FREE RENEE ROSE BOOKS?

Go to http://subscribepage.com/alphastemp to sign up for Renee Rose's newsletter and receive a free copy of *Alpha's Tempta-*

tion, Theirs to Protect, Owned by the Marine and more. In addition to the free stories, you will also get bonus epilogues, special pricing, exclusive previews and news of new releases.

FOREWORD

Dearest reader,

When the publishing rights to the *Alpha Doms* series returned to me from Stormy Night Publications, the original publisher, I considered a major re-edit / re-write, as I'd done with my *Made Men* series. It's been nearly ten years since *The Alpha's Hunger* was published, and my writing ability, style, and content have evolved significantly. I still love kink, but I've moved away from the punishy-style, keeping it more in the sexy realm.

In the end, I decided to leave the series as is—a picture in time. Humbling though it may be to me, by leaving it as is, you can see my evolution as a storyteller. *The Alpha's Hunger* (2015) is my billionaire boss wolf shifter 1.0., *Alpha's Temptation* (2017) became 2.0 and *Big Bad Boss* (2024) is 3.0. Who knows what shape 4.0 will take?

FOREWORD

As always, I am eternally grateful to you, the reader, who keeps me writing, pushing my craft, and learning to find new depth with each story I tell. Thank you for your readership now, and if you've been with me since the beginning, a million kisses for sticking with me all this time.

1

It started with a little lie. Just one.

Her alpha wolf, Ben, had had her wrists pinned over her head as he drove forcefully into her and he said something like, "Your body belongs to me, doesn't it?"

She had moaned, "Yes, sir," her eyes rolling back in her head with pleasure at being taken roughly.

"I'm going to come inside you today, Ash," he'd said.

"Yes, sir."

It hadn't mattered. She was on the pill—which he knew—but Ben Stone was a dom through and through and understood she liked to feel as though she had no choice. She had come with a scream, arching and shuddering beneath him and after he'd found his release, he'd lain down beside her, stroking a hand over her hip.

"I think we should make pups," he'd said, his breath warm against her ear. "Don't you?"

"Yes," she'd breathed. She would've said yes to anything he'd said at that moment. Post-coital murmurings probably shouldn't be counted as declarations of intent. And she hadn't realized he meant soon, as in 'let's start now.' They weren't even married yet. Not that human contracts meant much to him. As far as her shifter was concerned, he'd marked her and she was his. Forever.

The discussion about babies had been five months ago.

"I can't figure out how to talk to him about it," she confessed to her twin sister, Melissa, on the phone in her office. She lowered her voice, because even though a couple of walls separated her glass-windowed high-rise corporate office from Ben's, she never knew what he could hear with his super-human senses.

"Just tell him! This is getting stupid, Ash. If he thinks you guys are trying to get pregnant, and you're still taking the pill, it's dishonest. Is that the kind of marriage you want to have?"

"No," she said, resting her chin in her hand. "But he's going to be mad."

"Mad that you're not ready to have kids?"

"No... well, I don't know about that. Disappointed, probably. But definitely mad about the fact that I'm taking the pill." Her stomach knotted up thinking about it. There was no way out of the situation that she could see. If she talked to Ben, she risked his disappointment, or worse—anger. And he probably would decide she deserved punishment for her deceit. But she wasn't ready to have children. She was only twenty-five and Ben, the multi-millionaire CEO of Stone Technologies, had just given her a job as his personal assistant, which came with intoxicating power and excitement. So going off the pill was out of the question. She'd been around and around this circle of thoughts for the past five months without arriving at a solution.

"Ashley," Melissa said, affecting a stern tone. "You're being a coward."

She slumped in her chair. "I know."

"Go tell him right now."

Her insides twisted. "I can't."

"Now, Ashley. I'm serious. This is just stupid."

She exhaled. "Okay. You're right." She stood up. "I'm going."

"It will be fine."

"I don't think so."

"It will be. Call me and let me know how it goes."

"Okay-bye," she said all in one breath. She put the phone down and walked toward the door before she could chicken out.

The top floor of the building was busy, with upper level management holding meetings in their offices or talking on their phones. When she'd first come to this floor to interview, it had been dead silent, with just Ben and his secretary, Karen, occupying the space. He had kicked everyone else off the floor, preferring solitude in his grief over his brother's death.

She walked past Karen's desk. "Is he busy?" she asked.

"He's alone."

She tapped on the door and swung it open.

"Miss Bell," he said coolly, using the stern employer tone that made her panties wet. The green eyes that turned gold in wolf form surveyed her critically.

She walked in and shut the door. "Mr. Stone."

He leaned back in his chair, shoving his laptop back on his desk. His dark hair fell across his forehead, and he looked every bit the powerful Latin American millionaire, both in demeanor and stature. "You're late."

"I am?"

"Yes. I got hard for you an hour ago. Lock the door."

Her belly fluttered. She turned the lock on the handle. "I, um, wanted to talk to you about something."

He gave his head one decisive shake and she

shut her mouth. "Not now." He pointed at the floor at his feet. "Come over here."

Her nipples hardened in anticipation of whatever game he had in mind. But she needed to talk to him now, before she lost her nerve. "Ben?"

He arched a brow as if to ask whether she dared defy him.

She licked her lips and walked forward to the place he'd indicated.

"On your hands and knees. Facing away from me."

Okay… maybe she would tell him later. She lowered into position, her fitted work skirt and blouse making the stance seem all the more degrading.

Ben lifted the hem of her skirt, pulling it up to her waist.

She shivered.

He pulled her panties down to mid-thigh.

"What are you doing?" she asked.

"Quiet," he snapped, delivering a loud smack to the back of her right thigh. He knew she hated when he made noise like that, the idea of Karen or anyone else hearing their exploits too humiliating to contemplate. Everyone already assumed she'd slept her way to the top, and she'd be fighting that perception for years. "Do not speak unless you're spoken to."

Her pussy clenched. 'Yes, sir' rose to her lips

and she bit it back. She imagined what it would look like if someone walked in, and reminded herself she had locked the door. But what if she hadn't turned the knob the entire way? Or what if someone tried it and found it locked—they would know instantly what had been going on. Not that everyone didn't whisper about her anyway. That was part of why she didn't want to start a family yet. She had to prove herself here—prove she was more than Ben's eye candy, that she had a brain and could make good decisions.

But she lost all thought of anything work-related when the bulbous tip of something hard and plastic pushed against her sopping entrance. She jerked in surprise, then stilled, panting as Ben parted her inner lips with the toy and thrust it forward. He pushed it in, stretching her wide, then pulling it back out.

She gasped at the loss of sensation.

He repeated the action, fucking her with the toy.

She craned her neck to see over her shoulder, winning another sharp slap.

"Eyes on the floor."

"Yes, s—" Damn. She'd failed again.

He made a tsk-ing sound. "Disobedience will always be punished, Ashley. You know that."

She whimpered.

He ran a warm hand over her bottom. "Tonight

I'll give you a bare-bottomed spanking to teach you to mind," he said, relieving her fear that he would do it then and there, where others would hear. He rubbed the smooth plastic tip of the toy around the seam of her entrance, then thrust it inside her. It disappeared, small enough to fit in her greedy channel.

She heard the flick of a button and then her insides began to vibrate. She wobbled, her knees no longer holding her up, and she dropped her bottom toward her heels.

Ben's hand caught her ass before it reached its destination, sending her flying back into position with a yelp.

"Oh, God," she moaned, forgetting again not to speak.

"Naughty."

"I know," she moaned. "I'm sorry."

He chuckled. "You will be."

She shifted from one knee to the other, essentially wagging her tail in a growing desperation. The vibrator was too much—sensations overwhelming her and sending her over the edge, ready to orgasm at a moment's notice.

"Please, sir?" she whimpered.

"Put your chest and head down on the floor," he ordered.

She hesitated, the position so degrading she thought she ought to protest.

"One…"

She dropped into the described position before he reached two.

~

Ben admired his beautiful mate in the humiliating pose she'd assumed. Her head turned to one side, showing him her big blue eyes were already glassy. He loved to watch her lose control. He found her surrender intoxicating, her ready submission giving him a heady sense of masculine power.

"Reach back and hold your cheeks open." His voice had a roughened edge to it as his own need mounted.

"Ben—" she panted.

"Now, *mi amor*," he said firmly. "And you are to be seen and not heard."

"Oh, God," she moaned, clearly incapable of obeying this directive.

He smirked and watched as she reached back and gripped her own ass, pulling her twin globes apart to reveal her tight rosebud.

He opened a tube of lubricant and dropped a dollop from a foot in height, loving the way she jerked in surprise at the sensation.

I love you. Now was not the moment to say it, but he did. He adored Ashley Bell. Everything about her rocked his world—each day they spent together only deepening his need for her, his desire to take her ceaselessly never quenched. It was deeper than sex, though. Well, maybe not, because their sex was profound. But Ashley meant everything to him. She had wit, intelligence, and a generosity of heart he could never hope to imitate. She made him feel alive again after his brother's death. Or maybe for the first time ever.

Every time he told her about some terrible piece of his life, she swallowed it, accepting him, healing him, loving him.

He leaned forward in his office chair and touched her clenching rosette with the pad of his thumb, circling the tight ring of muscle. He gradually increased the pressure, stilling his movements. The moment she let him in, he retreated and replaced his thumb with the head of a second remote control bullet vibrator.

She mewled as he insisted, breaching her tight sphincter.

"No," she moaned. "Too much, too much, too much."

"Hush. I decide what's too much. You can take this. Be a good girl and open for me… just a little further to go."

As always, she obeyed him, her trust making him feel as tall as a mountain. He inserted the bullet all the way into her rectum, leaving just the cord outside to pull it out. Picking up the other remote control, he switched this one on as well.

She made an incoherent sound and collapsed on the floor, her knees splaying open.

He reached under her and brought the pad of his middle finger to her clit, circling it. "Don't come," he warned.

"Oh, God, please?" she wailed. She sounded close to tears, but he knew they were the ecstatic kind, the kind he loved to tease from her with too many orgasms or edging. "Please, you have to let me, sir. Oh, please, I'll do anything."

"Stand up."

She pumped her hips against the floor, as if hoping to find something to rub her clit against.

He slid his hand under and slapped her pussy several times, loving how dripping wet she'd become.

"Stand up," he repeated, giving a disapproving edge to his voice.

She scrambled to her feet, her hair disheveled, her cheeks flushed a pretty shade of pink.

He pulled her panties up, enjoying her expression of horror at being dismissed without reaching orgasm.

"No..." she murmured.

He pulled her skirt back down and smoothed it for her. Grasping her waist, he tugged her down, spinning her to sit on his lap with her back toward him. He stroked his hands down the tops of her legs, up the insides of her thighs to cup her mons.

She squirmed against him, trying to get off.

He slapped her panty-clad pussy. "Naughty."

"Oh, Ben," she whimpered.

He pinched her nipples, both at the same time—hard. "I want you to go back to your office and work on your reports." He turned off the vibrator in her pussy. "I will be using these intermittently on you today, but you do not have permission to climax. Do you understand?"

"No-o," she moaned.

He pinched her nipples harder, making her writhe. "Try it again."

"Yes, sir," she gasped. "Yes, I understand, but—"

"No buts. I want to keep you one stroke from an orgasm all day long. By the time I get you home and put my bareback cock inside you, you will orgasm so hard they'll hear you in Africa. And when you do, your sweet little pussy will take every drop of my semen up inside of you to fertilize that egg you should be dropping any day now."

She blushed, as she often did when he talked about getting her pregnant. He loved the thought of seeing her swollen with his child, starting the family he'd never known he wanted until he met her.

He switched off the anal vibrator. "You're dismissed," he said, giving her a wicked grin.

Her eyes watered, probably desperate for release, but she smoothed her hair and took a deep breath. "You're killing me," she whispered as she walked toward the door.

Oh, God. What was she going to do? That hadn't gone as planned. She couldn't think straight, her pussy still reverberating with the vibration of the toy he'd embedded in her. She tried to look professional, calm, and collected as she walked back to her office on wobbling knees.

Damn Ben Stone and his ability to turn her to a puddle of butter. Damn his sexy dark looks, authoritative command, and... tears sprang to her eyes once more. Damn his desire to start a family right now.

She opened the shades to her office window and looked out at the Denver skyline, the Rocky Mountains jutted majestically to the west. Maybe she should just give him what he wanted.

But what if she ended up resenting him and the child? What if she made a terrible stay-at-home mother and housewife? She didn't really think she could handle being stuck at home all day by herself with a couple of kids—no matter how much she loved them. She'd always pictured having children later in her life, in her thirties, after she'd established her career. And she hadn't really thought she'd stay home. Of course she and Ben hadn't really talked about whether he wanted her to stay home or not, but his sister-in-law was a stay-at-home mom, so she had a feeling that was the way the wolves did it. They were a rather old-fashioned patriarchal clan.

She sank into her office chair, hoping the moisture seeping from her pussy didn't soak through her panties onto her skirt. She leaned back and nibbled on her lip. To say she felt ashamed of herself was an understatement. She'd created quite a dilemma here, and the longer it went on, the worse it got.

She couldn't talk to Ben now. It would be impossible.

She surged to her feet as the vibrator in her rectum came to life. Oh, dear lord. How would she survive this day? She looked at the clock as she gingerly lowered herself back down on her buzzing bottom. Only ten a.m. She would die before quitting time.

He turned on first one vibrator, then the other, and alternated for a solid thirty minutes before the lunch hour. When he stepped into her office to take her to lunch, he realized she wouldn't make it through the day.

She looked feverish, her eyes wild and dilated, her lips pursed with tension. Her thick, reddish-brown hair looked rumpled, as if she'd been running her hands through it.

He would take her home, fuck her, and give her the afternoon off. "Come, *mi amor*. Get your purse, I'm taking you to lunch."

She looked confused, as if the simple task of picking up her purse was too much to comprehend.

He grabbed it for her and helped her to her feet. "Come on, sweetheart. I'm almost through with you," he whispered in her ear.

She slumped against him, clearly relieved.

He slid an arm around her waist to provide support and led her out. "Ashley isn't feeling well, so I'm taking her home. I'm not sure whether I'll be back," he told Karen.

"Thank you, sir," she said.

In the elevator, he flipped the switch on both vibrators, watching the torment bloom on Ashley's face as he pushed her up against the wall and wedged one thigh between her legs. She whimpered and ground her mons on him. He cupped her ass and squeezed, savoring the feel of her muscled buns.

"I think you would have called the fire department if I left you until quitting time," he murmured in her ear.

She bit his neck, which kicked his wolf senses into high gear, his teeth lengthening and his vision doming as his eyes turned yellow. The elevator dinged and they sprang apart as several people got on the elevator. He switched the vibrators off.

"Good afternoon, Mr. Stone," said a man he recognized but whose name and position he couldn't recall.

He nodded to him without answering.

"Hi, Charlie, how are things in R&D?" Ashley asked, playing her part of personal assistant perfectly. She'd been pushing him to foster better relationships with his employees and she somehow seemed to know every one of them.

Charlie lit up at the recognition. "Great," he said, looking to Ben. "We're finished with the prototype Superstation. Would you like to test it out?"

He didn't answer. His old leadership habit had been to keep everyone out—to refuse to interact unless absolutely necessary. Now, he knew he had to if he wanted to improve morale, but he didn't know how far to go. If he wasn't careful, he'd get pulled in a million directions.

"Mr. Stone's schedule is tight this week, but if you email me, I'll set up thirty minutes next week for you to show him everything."

Charlie looked slightly flustered, as if he didn't

know whether he'd been put off or not, but he bobbed his head. "Okay, sounds great."

"You have my email, right?"

"Uh… Ashleybell@stonetech.com?"

Ashley gave Charlie one of her megawatt smiles, which caused a growl to rise in Ben's throat. "That's right," she said cheerfully as the elevator stopped again and the doors slid open.

"Okay, thanks," Charlie said, backing out, looking from one to the other of them, a bit dazedly.

The doors closed and he took Ashley's hand and gave it a squeeze.

"You growled."

"No," he denied it. He had almost growled.

"I heard it, wolf. What gives?"

"Wolves give notice of their property when another male is looking." He watched the effect of his politically incorrect statement on Ashley's nipples as she tried to muster indignation. "And I'm mostly wolf right now," he admitted in a rough voice.

She smiled at that, pressing against him, the lust shining in her eyes.

The elevator stopped on their parking garage floor and he scooped her into his arms, carrying her out.

She shrieked. "Stop, someone will see."

"I don't care," he said, too far gone into what

she called Neanderthal mode. She was his. It was time to drag her back to the cave and have his way with her. He flicked on the pussy vibrator, chuckling as she jerked and crossed her legs, trying to rub them together for more friction.

He opened the passenger side door to his black Mustang and settled her in, flicking on the anal bullet just before he buckled her seatbelt.

She arched and her hands shot to her sex, her pelvis undulating to meet her fingers.

"Ah, ah," he said, prying them away and placing them on the dash. "I didn't give you permission to touch yourself. Your pleasure is at my discretion, remember?"

She moaned, closing her eyes and rolling her head back and forth on the backrest.

He chuckled, shutting the door. As he got in the driver's seat, he flipped off the pussy vibrator.

"Please," she whimpered. "Ben, I can't take this." Tears of sexual frustration edged from the outer corners of her eyes.

As always, the scent of his mate's tears subdued him, even though rationally, he knew they were a sign of her imminent pleasure, not harm. Still, his instincts screamed for him to fix it, and he flicked off the anal vibrator as well.

Her moan was one of disappointment this time.

"I know, *mi amor*. I'm going to take care of all of your needs as soon as I get you home."

She turned her head and blinked at him as if seeing through a haze. "I love you, Ben Stone," she murmured.

Something more powerful even than lust rocked him, puffing up his chest with warmth. "I love you, too, *mi reina*."

When he pulled up in the driveway of the house they'd rented while they had their dream house built, Ashley opened the car door and bolted for the house. He chuckled, throwing open his own door and giving chase. He caught her fumbling with the keys. Yanking them from her hands, he managed to open the door and half-carried, half-dragged her inside, tearing her clothes off as he went.

He flicked on one vibrator, then the other. He'd stripped Ashley out of her sexy skirt and jacket and had her blouse halfway unbuttoned as he pushed her backward toward the bedroom. Blouse off. Bra unhooked. He picked her up and tossed her onto the bed, pouncing over her.

Panties down.

He pulled the pussy vibe out of her dripping cunt without bothering to turn it off.

She reached for the button on his pants and undid it, freeing his length as he claimed her mouth. He wanted to devour her, eat her alive. His teeth had lengthened, his vision had sharpened, which meant his eyes had changed from green to gold. He licked into her mouth, holding back the growl of domination that rose in his throat.

Not that Ashley ever protested when he took her roughly.

ASHLEY THOUGHT she would die if she didn't come. The vibration in her ass had turned her to jelly, her body quivering for Ben. "Please," she whispered when he broke their kiss. She had his shirt in her fist, and she pulled it toward her, trying to drive despite the fact that she was on the bottom.

Thankfully, Ben let her. He took her with one penetrating stroke, entering to the hilt and staying there while she squirmed under him. She wrapped her legs around his back to pull him in deeper, lifting her hips to move him inside her.

Ben palmed the place where her neck met shoulder, holding her in place as he withdrew and entered once more, with force.

She moaned wantonly. "I need you... I need you, please."

Ben's mouth stretched into a wolfish grin, his teeth gleaming dangerously. He backed out and slammed in again, his eyes glittering gold, his expression hungry. He reached toward his pants still around his legs and she thought he would pull them off, but instead he retrieved a small electronic device.

Suddenly, the rate of vibration in her ass increased. She screamed, shoving her pelvis against him, trying desperately to get relief. Ben thankfully began to thrust inside her, shoving all the way in with a bone-jolting force.

"Oh, God, yes. Please…"

"I love it when you beg," he murmured, his voice thick. He slammed into her again and again, taking her with the violence she craved, each stroke too much, too hard, each withdrawal too soon.

It seemed her entire body split open to him, her heart burst wide, her body completely his. She no longer squirmed or writhed or tried to direct the action, because working against him would have painful results. She gave herself over to him completely, his ragdoll, his marked mate, open for his seed.

"Come for me, Ashley," he said in a guttural tone and slammed deeply inside at the same moment he tugged the cord for the anal vibrator, pulling it through the tight ring of her sphincter muscles and leaving it halfway out, stretching her wide with its buzzing girth. She shattered, her pussy clenching, her internal muscles contracting in wave after wave of mind-blowing release. It seemed to go on forever—both his orgasm and hers. She swore she felt the searing heat of his cum inside her, sensed the way her body joyfully received it, milking his cock and propelling it deep inside her. When at last, her muscles stopped their fluttering, Ben eased the vibrator the rest of the way out, but left his enormous cock inside her.

Without a doubt, this was the perfect way to make a baby. It had been a nearly religious experience and the euphoria flowing through her now was only interrupted by one thought: she'd screwed everything up.

Because of her deceit, there would be no wolf pup conceived that day. The pill would prevent it, and her soon-to-be husband had no idea of her sabotage.

She turned her head to the side as hot tears leaked from her eyes.

Ben kissed them away, the tenderness of his response only making her feel worse. He thought they were from the incredible orgasm, not the wracking guilt that darkened her chest. Easing out and settling beside her, he pulled her into his arms, kissing her face and hair, nibbling on her ear. "*Te quiero… te amo.*"

More tears. "I love you, too, Ben."

He held her until her body stopped trembling and their temperature returned to normal.

"I'm going to go to the restroom and then I'll make us some lunch," she murmured, slipping out of his embrace. In the bathroom, she unzipped the cosmetic bag where she hid the pills and stared at them with disgust. Her stomach clenched and she wanted to throw up. If only she could throw up the half month's worth she'd already taken. She wondered what would happen if she stopped taking them today. Was there still a chance for pregnancy? And if so, would the baby be healthy, or would the pills cause some abnormality?

The sound of the door opening behind her made her jump and gasp, yanking her hand with the pills behind her back as she spun to face Ben.

He froze.

It was stupid to try to trick him—he had shifter instincts she couldn't understand. His hearing and eyesight were ten times better than hers.

His expression showed nothing, but any doubt she had of whether he saw something faded when he said in a deadly voice, "What's that, Ash?"

Tears of shame immediately spilled from her eyes as she reluctantly brought her hand forth to show him. "I'm sorry," she said, spreading her fingers to show him the pills.

He stared, a look of disbelief clouding his face. "What is that?" he repeated.

He was going to make her say it. She couldn't meet his eyes. Staring at the pills, she repeated, "I'm sorry, Ben." Her voice cracked on the words. "I've been lying to you. I—I just didn't know if I was ready to have children."

Ben hadn't moved. He stood deathly still. "Why lie?"

More tears spilled down her cheeks. "I just—" Her shoulders sagged. "The first time you brought it up, I wasn't really thinking straight and after that... I don't know. I was a coward, I guess. I was afraid."

He took a step—not toward her, but backwards. "You were afraid of me?" His voice was so quiet, so devoid of emotion, like the blankness on his face, that it frightened her.

"Ben—" She stopped. What else was there to say? She had no excuse, no explanation for a deceit she'd allowed to go on for far too long for him to forgive. "I'm sorry," she whispered.

He turned away, peeling off his shirt as he walked away. Which meant he was going to shift. She stood in the bathroom door, watching as he shed his pants in the hallway and transformed with liquid grace into an enormous black wolf.

"Ben," she called out, inanely.

He didn't turn to look back before he nosed out the dog door, disappearing.

The house had never felt so hollow.

2

Ben couldn't believe it. He loped off, up into the foothills, his mind and body numb. They had purposely rented a house near the wilderness so he could roam at will in wolf form, and he ran up the steep side of a mountain face now, wanting to run forever.

Ashley had lied to him. She'd betrayed his trust. But even worse, it had been because she was afraid to tell him the truth. That fact had hit him like a fist in the gut. What kind of mate was he if his female couldn't even talk to him about the things that were important to her?

Because he'd never witnessed an ounce of cowardice in Ashley. Even as a human, she had alpha female written all over her—confident, whip-smart, and a social genius. She could wrap anyone around her finger. She'd dared joke with him on her interview, even though she'd been nervous. And she'd kept opening her heart to him, when he'd repeatedly shut her down.

So to hear she feared him meant she hadn't forgiven him or forgotten the way he'd marked her. It meant they didn't have any level of trust between them.

Images of his mother, cowering from his father's wrath, flashed before his eyes. He ran faster, over the rocky terrain, the cold February wind blowing through his fur. He'd always feared he'd become his father. It was why he hadn't wanted to lead his brother's pack, and hadn't looked for a mate. But you can't escape your parentage, it seemed.

The loving, trusting relationship his brother so easily modeled with his wife and he'd foolishly thought he might find with Ashley was not for wolves like him. The gray day turned colder, the higher he climbed. Time and distance fell away and he reached the tree line, where snow still covered the ground. Fresh snow began to fall.

He stopped, turning in a circle to scent the air. He smelled elk, but was in no mood to hunt. Sitting, he lifted his nose to the sky and howled, a long, mournful howl.

Only a toothbrush would get out the dirt between the grout lines of the shower. Ashley pushed her sleeves up and returned to her position on her hands and knees in the empty bathtub, scrubbing at the tiles. She'd attacked the house, cleaning it from top to bottom, as if that somehow might make things right with Ben. It was now pushing six o'clock and he hadn't returned. Her stomach had clenched like a fist.

When she finished cleaning, she grilled three steaks and made a Greek salad and herbed quinoa.

Still he didn't come home. The clock read half past eight. Night had come and snowflakes had begun to fall. Surely the cold didn't bother him. But even so, was it a sign of how upset he was that he didn't return, despite the dark and cold?

Unable to eat, she dished the food onto plates, covered them with plastic wrap and put them in the refrigerator. The house didn't feel like hers anymore. She tiptoed around it, like she didn't belong, every creak of the wood floors making her jump. Wrapping a blanket around her shoulders, she sat down and turned on the television, flipping through the channels. She found an old Clint Eastwood movie and watched it until her eyelids began to droop.

Maybe she should just go to bed. But would he return soon? Or had he gone elsewhere for the night? Was this the end for them? Tears pricked her eyes, but she blinked them back, heading to their bedroom to try to sleep.

She woke at two a.m. to find the space beside her in the bed still empty. A sense of dread filled her chest as she climbed out of bed to check the house. She stopped in the living room, finding Ben's sleeping form sprawled on the couch. He was naked, as if he'd just shifted back. The chiseled muscles of his powerful chest and arms were exposed, with a light blanket tossed over his waist.

They weren't sleeping together?

She willed herself to exhale, but couldn't seem to catch her breath. Did this mean things were over between them? Her nose burned as tears crowded up into her throat. She crept to the side of the couch and knelt down beside Ben's face, tears spilling down her cheeks.

His eyes blinked open and he sat up. "Ashley," he said in a hoarse voice. "Go to sleep."

"I can't," she said. She remembered he'd told her once that the smell of her tears would bring him to his knees. She thought she saw pain in his eyes, but in the darkness, it was hard to tell. "Can we talk?" she croaked.

He sighed. "We'll talk tomorrow."

"Will you come to bed?"

"No," he said heavily. "I don't think so."

"Then I'm staying here," she said, brushing the tears with the back of her hand.

"No," he said, his voice hardening. "Go back to bed. Now."

She shook her head.

He made a sound of irritation and reached for her, freezing when she flinched. "You're afraid of me," he said hollowly.

She opened her mouth, then closed it, unsure how to answer. Had she flinched because she was scared? No, not really. Rationally, she wasn't afraid of Ben, but his dominance did have an effect on her, making her instincts for self-preservation kick in, just as seeing him in wolf form always made her gulp.

"That's why you felt you had to lie to me."

She shook her head. "I just… I didn't want to disappoint you at first. And then, once the lie was out, I was afraid to confess the truth because I knew you'd be mad—rightfully so."

"Did you think I'd force you into parenting? That you don't have a say in the matter?"

"No… no. But you seemed so excited. And I—"

He waited when she trailed off.

"My career is just getting started. I love working for you and I'm just not willing to give that up yet."

"This is the discussion we should have had five months ago."

She dropped her head and stared at the outline of her hands in the dark. "I know."

"I wouldn't have pushed you," he said, a bitter edge to his voice. "I thought you wanted this."

"I do," she protested. "Just maybe not right this second. We're not even married yet." She knew the institution of marriage didn't matter to shifters the way it did to humans, but they had agreed to have a long engagement to give her and her family time to adjust to the suddenness of their relationship. In Ben's world, he'd marked her and she belonged to him, period. She had accepted that, but still wanted time to get used to the idea.

"I'll stop taking the pill. I was going to throw them out today, when you caught me."

He made an impatient gesture. "You don't have to. I don't care about that. You think pups are more important to me than your happiness?"

Shame made her face grow hot and her eyes wet again. "I'm sorry."

He said nothing.

"Are you going to punish me?"

"No."

"Why not?"

"Go to bed, Ashley," he said, sounding tired.

"Not without you."

He reached for her again and this time she held still, not surprised to find his touch gentle, despite the stony lines of his face. He scooped her into his arms and carried her to the bedroom, where he tried to deposit her on the bed. She clung to his neck, though, refusing to let go.

He growled and she nearly let go, but rallied her courage to prove she wasn't afraid of him. He dropped to the bed with her and held her down, delivering several sharp smacks to her pajama-clad backside.

She lay perfectly still for them, holding her breath. A spanking really would clear the air between them. He'd given her a serious spanking once before, and while it had hurt and she hadn't enjoyed it, it had brought them closer.

He didn't continue to spank her though, nor did he leave. He settled beside her on his back, his fingers knit behind his head, looking up at the ceiling.

She would take what she could. Curling against his body, she tucked her face against his side and closed her eyes, praying he'd find it in his heart to forgive her.

ASHLEY RADIATED ANXIETY. It sent his shifter instincts haywire to feel his mate's stress, and yet he couldn't manage to change his own emotions, which largely seemed dead. He'd returned to the way he'd been before he met her—the 'Stone man' who lacked emotion, fired people at will, and never smiled. He took her hand in the elevator, making an attempt to soothe her.

She looked up at him with her big blue eyes, the pleading quality twisting his heart. The elevator stopped and the doors slid open for other employees to get on. Ashley moved to pull her hand away, but he held it fast, tugging her slightly behind him to hide their clasp. He did not release her until they reached the top floor and they parted without speaking. He'd never been a man of many words, but even to him, the silence seemed strange. The gulf between just seemed to grow with each passing moment.

He wasn't angry. Betrayed, yes, and he felt like an idiot for the months he'd thought they were trying to conceive a child while she'd been taking the pill. The lack of trust between them devastated him. He wasn't the type to trust or love easily, but when he'd taken Ashley as his mate, he'd thought he'd turned a corner. Now, he could practically feel his old walls re-erecting themselves around his heart.

Worse, he couldn't stop thinking about Ashley's fear of him. Maybe mating with a human couldn't work. The difference in their physical abilities would always separate them. Shifters have a pack order. Dominance is established and maintained with physical expressions. Males resolve problems with other males with a fight. They resolve problems with a female by spanking. Ashley hadn't minded it—hell, she loved it when he flexed his authority, but even so, she must worry he'd lose control as he had when he'd marked her, causing her real injury and harm.

He didn't hear from her until lunchtime, when she tapped on his door and entered. Usually her smile and her presence brightened his days. Today, she looked diminished, almost shy—which didn't fit her outgoing personality. He hated seeing her that way.

"Do you want to get lunch? Or, um, do you want me to get you something?"

He didn't want to go to lunch with her. Just seeing her pained him. "Bring me a sandwich," he said, not meaning to sound so curt.

She ducked her head and nodded, leaving without a word.

Damn. Why did he have such a talent at making things worse?

She brought him the sandwich, and he ate alone at his desk. He poured himself into financial reports for the rest of the day, not surfacing until six o'clock, when he closed up his office and found Ashley slumped in her chair, staring at her computer screen.

"You ready?" he asked.

She looked disappointed, as if she'd hoped he

would say something else. But what was there to say?

They walked in silence to the elevator. Once inside, he put an arm around her and pulled her to his side, where she melted against him. He bent to kiss the top of her head.

She lifted her eyes. "Are we okay?"

"Yeah," he said, but they both knew it was a lie.

At home, she went to the kitchen and began to reheat the dinner she'd made for them the night before. He took off his jacket and tie and unbuttoned his shirt at the collar. From the kitchen, he smelled steak, but also the salty smell of Ashley's tears.

Nothing subdues a shifter more than the scent of his mate's anguish. Damn. He walked into the kitchen to find Ashley facing the stove, her shoulders hunched and tears running down her face.

"Hey," he said softly, turning her around. "Enough." He wiped the tears from her face. "That's not helping anything."

"What will?" she asked, her voice rising to the pitch of desperation. "Because I can't stand this living with a stranger thing we have going at the moment. Why won't you just yell at me? Or punish me? Aren't you the alpha around here?" She gave him an ineffectual shove, her face screwed up into a little ball of fury.

"Enough," he said, lacing his voice with the hard edge of authority.

"Is it?" She slapped his chest with the palm of her hand.

Even knowing she meant to goad him into it, he responded instinctively, as any dominant wolf did when challenged, catching her wrist and spinning her around to pin it behind her back. He delivered the first swat before he had a chance to think.

He stopped, inhaling deeply. He didn't want this. If she feared him, spanking her didn't help. But then she'd practically begged him for it. Maybe she needed it, to assuage her guilt. She certainly wasn't fighting him now, standing perfectly still, her head bent forward so her thick hair curtained her face.

He released her and turned her to face the living room. "Take off your clothes and kneel in the corner over there," he said, pointing to the one near the couch.

She moved immediately, not meeting his eye, her head still bowed submissively.

He remained where he was, conflicted. It was too late to change his mind, of course. But what if punishing her only made things worse between them? He shut off the oven, leaving the steaks inside to stay warm.

When he turned, Ashley had taken her position. He caught his breath at the sight—her long reddish-brown hair falling down her back, the flare of her hips and, of course, her perfect ass, settled between her heels where she knelt. His cock forgot his reluctance to punish her, pressing eagerly against his trousers.

He walked over to the couch and sat down. "Come, Ashley."

"Woof," she said, barely louder than a whisper, wringing a half-smile from him. It had been her joke since the day he interviewed her and had told her to sit. He hadn't laughed then, and yet she'd persisted, just as she'd persevered despite his repeated rejections of her affection.

She walked to stand in front of him, her chin dropped, hands clasped behind her back.

"Why am I punishing you?"

"For—" She cleared her throat. "For lying."

He waited.

"—sir," she added.

He said nothing, keeping his face blank.

She nibbled her lip. "I should have known you would listen to and value my feelings on the matter. You always have."

Her words came as a relief to him.

"Ben?"

He raised an eyebrow expectantly.

"Would you make me stay home with the kids?"

He grabbed her waist and pulled her to sit on his lap. "Make you?" he asked. "Is that how you think things work around here?"

She fidgeted with her hands.

Taking her chin, he lifted her face to his.

"I don't know. It's just—your sister-in-law…"

"That's what Shayla wanted. She never had an interest in getting involved with Leon's company; that's why he left it to me. Shayla wanted to be well cared for, so she could devote herself to her children." He studied Ashley's blue eyes. "Did you think it was a shifter thing? Is that what this is about?"

She shrugged. "Well, it's part of my fear. But also I'm just not ready."

He nodded slowly. "Look, I know I've been an asshole. I ran Stone Tech like a dictator, and it was my way or the highway. But with you—" He broke off, his throat closing with emotion. "You expected more of me, you believed I had a heart. With you, I thought I'd changed."

Ashley's lip trembled.

"Don't make me into that guy again. Do you really think I'd make you do anything that made you unhappy?"

A tear spilled down her cheek and he thumbed it away. "No. I'm sorry," she whispered. "I'm really sorry."

Ben lifted her from his lap, deftly turning her face down over it, her bare bottom angled perfectly for his punishment. Goosebumps raised on her flesh. She reached for one of the throw pillows, wrapping her arms around it. The first few spanks stung the worst, the shock so much more than what she expected.

She realized how much he held back when he spanked her in fun, because each slap of his hand connected now with force enough to make her lose her breath. She meant to hold still, but found herself twisting and bucking, trying to wriggle her way off his lap. He wrapped his arm around her waist and pulled her close.

"Do not kick or I'll take off my belt," he warned.

She crossed her ankles, squeezing them together to keep from kicking. The warning actually came as a relief—it meant he hadn't planned on using the belt later. Not that it mattered at the moment, his hand was doing enough damage. It came raining down swift and hard, first one cheek, then the other, then square in the middle.

She clamped her lips together to keep from crying out as he spanked her over and over again. She buried her head in the couch cushions, biting at the fabric. "Ow… please," she found herself begging, despite her resolve to take it like a good girl.

Firm smacks continued to fall, the burn setting in from the previous ones making it all the worse.

"Ben... oh! Please," she whimpered, her cheeks throbbing now as he continued to spank her ceaselessly.

He stopped, resting his hand on her heated flesh. "How many months did you let me believe we were trying to conceive a child, Ashley?"

She cringed, her shame worse than the pain. "Five months," she mumbled into the sofa.

"How many?" he asked sharply.

She turned her head to speak. "Five, sir."

He began to spank her again, just as hard and fast as before.

She moaned and squirmed, reaching back to try to rub.

He caught her wrist and bent it behind her back. "You know better than that, little girl," he said in his most stern and disapproving tone.

She hunched her shoulders against the agonizing smacks. "I'm sor-ry," she wailed.

Thankfully, he stopped again. "Five months of deceit deserves five spankings, don't you think?"

"Tonight?" she asked, suddenly terrified.

He chuckled. "Not tonight."

"When?"

"When I decide."

He lifted her to her feet and she cupped her flaming ass. "This spanking isn't done," he warned.

"Go stand in the corner while I get something from the kitchen."

She walked to the corner, trying to rub away the burn.

"No rubbing," Ben called from the kitchen. "Interlace your fingers on top of your head."

She sighed and obeyed, feeling like a very naughty girl who had already been well chastised. What more did he plan to do?

She listened to the sounds of him rummaging in the kitchen and then his return to the living room. His footsteps sounded behind her.

"Bend over and grab your ankles," he said, tugging her hips backward to give her room to fold.

She swallowed, her mouth dry.

He waited for her to comply, watching her slowly bending at the waist and reaching toward the floor. The stretching of her ass only made the throbbing worse. He pressed something slick and cool against her anus and she jerked, trying to clamp her cheeks closed. The position kept her spread to him, though, and he pushed more insistently, until she relaxed and allowed it in.

"You may stand up now," he said, wiggling the object inside her. Turning her hips, he used the intrusive object to propel her forward, until she reached the arm of the sofa. "Bend over," he said, pressing her torso down. "This is ginger," he said. "You're going to keep it in for the remainder of your spanking. I'm going to make sure your bottom burns on the outside and in," he said.

She tried to erect herself, craning her neck around to look, but Ben pushed her back down and held her in place.

"If you're a good girl, I will finish this spanking with my hand," he said. "That means no reaching and no kicking. If you're naughty, I will take off my belt and spank you until you scream. Understand?"

Her heart thundered in her chest. "Yes, sir," she whispered, her pussy clenching despite her fear.

His fist wrapped in her hair and he tugged her head back. "You like it when I punish you," he growled in her ear, probably smelling the scent of her arousal.

Her nipples hardened. The roughness in his voice gave away his desire for her. Her wolf had returned from whatever cold place he'd retreated.

"I don't like it," she said, which was a half-truth.

He pulled her hair back again. "Yes, you do."

"I don't like disappointing you." That was all true.

His teeth closed lightly on her shoulder, then released—a love bite.

She became aware of a burning from the ginger and she moaned. "It burns."

He released her hair and pushed her back down. "It's supposed to burn. I'm teaching you a lesson, little girl. Do you lie to me?"

"No, sir," she said, gulping as he began to spank her again, just as hard as he had before. This time, her ass was already sore and now her anus burned as well. She tightened around it, which only made it worse.

Ben spanked and spanked, merciless in his punishment as she lay helplessly sprawled over the arm of the sofa with a stick of ginger in her ass. Her entire body grew hot from the root, and she began to sweat. Her pussy swelled between her legs, heating along with her entire pelvis, arousal dripping down her legs.

"Oh, it burns... it burns," she moaned. Every time she shifted or squeezed, she incited a fresh bloom of agony from the ginger root. That, combined with the pain of his seemingly endless spanking seemed more than she could bear. "Ben," she whimpered. "I'm sorry. I'm so sorry. I'll be a good girl," she pleaded. "I'll never lie again. Please don't spank me, please don't—"

"Shh." The spanking stopped. Ben slid a finger between her legs, over her glossy slit.

"Please take it out," she begged.

"No," he said. "I'm going to fuck you with it in."

Her pussy clenched, eager for any activity he wanted to give her.

His finger had found her clit, circling the sensitive nub.

She heard his zipper and spread her legs, arching her back.

He pushed the ginger in deeper, creating a fresh zing of torturous burn and gave her bottom several more smacks. "You may not come," he said at the same time he stretched her wide with his thick cock.

"What?" she asked, confused.

"You heard me, little girl. You were naughty and are being punished. I don't think you deserve to come tonight."

She couldn't believe it. Not coming would be an impossibility. She'd almost just come from him saying he was going to fuck her. And yet, disobeying him, tonight of all nights, seemed out of the question.

"Ben," she whimpered. "Please... I need to come."

He slid his cock in and out of her, shoving the ginger deeper with each in-stroke. The burning was unbearable and her need so great she thought she'd explode.

"No."

He gripped her waist and picked up speed, pumping harder.

She surrendered, offering herself up to him, trying to forget about the pain and her mounting desperation to come.

BEN BURIED himself deep inside Ashley, his release pouring out. He wrapped his arms around her from behind, lifting her torso and nuzzling at her neck. He'd been a fool. Ashley had been right, as usual. A spanking did fix everything. Or at least it had brought them back together, to face their challenges as a couple, rather than two islands drifting apart.

He cupped her breasts in his hands, rolling his thumbs over her nipples.

She moaned wantonly.

He eased out of her and pulled the ginger finger from her ass. "Don't get dressed," he murmured in her ear. "I want you to serve me dinner just as you are."

She turned in his arms, resting her hands on his chest and looking up at him shyly.

He bent to kiss her, claiming her mouth with great authority, sliding his tongue between her lips, showing her with action what he had trouble expressing.

When they broke apart, he saw her relief. She understood she'd been forgiven and that all was right between them. He stepped back to allow her passage. "Go on," he said, giving her reddened ass a slap as she turned toward the kitchen.

He raised the temperature on the thermostat so she wouldn't get cold prancing around their kitchen in the nude and settled in a chair to watch, his cock already forgetting its recent release.

Ashley's hands slid over her swollen cheeks, circling and rubbing away the sting. He hoped he hadn't spanked hard enough to leave marks. As reluctant as he'd been to begin with, once he started spanking, his emotions had cleared. Her willingness to accept his displeasure in that form eased all his discontent, leaving him in appreciation of her beautiful submission.

Now, as she dished salads onto their plates and pulled steaks and quinoa out of the oven, her eyes were bright with unspent desire, face still flushed. She darted glances at him under her lashes, sending a fresh shot of lust kicking through him every time.

"It's ready," she murmured, turning to face him.

He gave her a lazy grin and unfolded himself from the chair, walking to the table. "*Gracias, mi amor.*"

She set the plates down at their separate places, but before she could sit, he grasped her waist and tugged her down to sit on his lap. She flinched a little at the contact of her chafed bottom with his pants, but then snuggled in.

"You eat here tonight."

"Okay," she said, sounding pleased.

He picked up his knife and cut her a piece of steak, which had turned slightly dry from being reheated.

"I'm sorry," she said. "It was better yesterday."

He stabbed it with his fork and lifted it to her

full lips. "It's fine," he reassured her. "And it was my own fault, so don't apologize."

She chewed, her hair falling forward to cover part of her face.

He brushed it away, watching her eat.

"I want to have your babies," she said when she swallowed.

He suppressed a smile. "Too bad. You had your chance and you blew it."

Her ocean-blue eyes studied his face. "I threw out the pills."

He sobered, his chest growing heavy again over this conflict that never should have been an issue. "Ash… baby. I'm not asking you to have my pups. I thought you wanted them now and I ran with it. It turned me on to think about getting you pregnant. But I can wait—I never meant to pressure you."

"I know," she said, touching his lips with the pad of her index finger. "But I realized that you… that our family is more important than my career."

He picked up her fingers and kissed them. "You're going back on the pill," he said, adding steel to his voice so she'd know his decision was final. "We will re-evaluate in a year. Understood?"

Her eyes watered and she nodded. "Yes, sir."

"Good girl." He popped another bite of steak into her mouth.

He continued to feed her as he stroked her soft

skin and enjoyed the view of her perfect breasts bouncing near his face.

When they'd finished, he helped her clean up the kitchen, then scooped her up and carried her to their bed, where he laid her on her front. Her bottom was still red, her pussy still gleaming wet between her thighs. He stroked her bottom, squeezing her sore cheeks.

"Mmm," she encouraged.

He crawled on top of her, unbuttoning his shirt. "The trouble with naughty girls like you is that you like your spankings too much," he said, fisting her hair and tugging her head to the side to bite her shoulder. "I have to be very firm to make an impression. Isn't that right?"

She whimpered, probably not knowing how to answer such a question.

He divested himself of his shirt and undershirt, then unbuttoned his pants and slid them off. "You may please me now," he said, settling beside her on his back.

She scrambled up to her hands and knees, crawling over him with an eagerness that had his cock standing at full mast before she even arrived. She licked her lips as she reached for his shaft, then bent her head down and flicked her tongue on the underside of his glans.

He shuddered with pleasure, thrusting his hips up for more.

She gave him a Cheshire cat smile, lowering her eyelids seductively and opening her mouth to engulf the head of his cock.

He reached for her, burying his fingers in her thick, glossy hair as she lowered and lifted her head over his shaft. She sucked hard, moving her tongue in a swirling motion than made him dizzy with desire.

"Bring your ass over here," he said, his voice thick.

She turned sideways, offering him her punished bottom as she continued to expertly tease his cock with her tongue.

He brought his hand crashing down on her bottom, causing her to surge forward and deep-throat his cock. "I'll tell you what, little girl. You're doing such a good job sucking my cock that I might let you come. But I'm not going to touch that pretty little pussy of yours. All I'm going to do is spank your rosy red ass. Do you think you can come from a spanking alone?"

She made a sound around his cock, the vibration sending a zing of pleasure straight through to his toes.

He slapped her again. "Was that a yes?"

She popped off him. "Yes, sir."

Another spank, harder this time. "Did I say you could stop what you're doing?"

"No, sir," she said, returning to her ministrations.

He spanked slowly, deliberately. Not too hard, but not softly, either. He aimed for the middle of her cheeks, just above her sex.

Judging by the enthusiasm with which she applied herself to his throbbing shaft, he knew she was getting close. He let his hand fall again and again as she bobbed frantically over him, humming and sucking. Seeing her come apart was his undoing. His balls contracted.

"I'm coming," he warned her, but she didn't stop. He continued to spank her, faster now, wondering if she'd be able to do it. She wiggled her hips, rolling them around, begging to be fucked, but he resisted touching her except to spank. He came and she paused, receiving his seed in her mouth, her hand wrapped tightly around the base of his cock.

She sat up and swallowed, giving Ben her wild-eyed look.

He sat up and pulled her across his lap, resuming the spanking.

She parted her legs, angling her bottom up, lifting it to meet his hand. Fingers twisting into the bedspread, she arched, teeth bared like a little wildcat.

"Only the naughtiest girls can come just from having their sore, red bottoms spanked."

She cried out, squeezing her legs together and rubbing her hips over his lap, her bottom clenched tight and toes pointed straight out behind her.

He chuckled, squeezing her tightened buns and shaking. "That's my girl," he murmured. "I knew you could do it."

She lifted her head from her arms, looking exhausted. "Does that count as one of my spankings?"

He threw his head back and laughed. "Yes. But don't imagine they will all be this pleasurable."

3

The phone on Ashley's desk rang, the display reading Ben's extension.

"Hi," she said, breathless.

"Miss Bell, I need to see you in my office right away," he said.

A shiver of excitement zipped through her. "Yes, Mr. Stone," she said and hung up. She loved it when he played stern boss with her.

She walked past his secretary, giving her a nod, and entered his office.

"Shut the door," he said, "and lock it." As usual, his face gave away nothing.

She turned the lock, excitement warring with concern. Was he going to spank her in here? And risk Karen or others hearing?

As if to answer her unspoken question, he stood and pointed at his desk. "Bend over," he said.

She hesitated long enough to earn an arched brow, which launched her into action. Even if they were playing a game, she had no desire to earn his disapproval. Not after everything that had happened.

She stepped up to his desk and bent over, placing her hands on the walnut surface.

He came around to stand behind her and his fingertips brushed her thighs, sending a jolt of electricity through her. He found the hem of her skirt and pulled it up slowly until it bunched around her waist.

He had spanked her in his office before, but he'd left her panties up to keep from making any sound. This time, though, he peeled them down to mid-thigh.

Her tummy fluttered.

"Have you ever heard of a loopy johnny, Ashley?"

"No—" She cleared her throat. "No, sir."

He slid an implement in front of her on the desk. It had a wooden handle, wrapped in leather, and three loops of thin black cord extending from the handle.

She shivered.

"It's supposed to be one of the quietest implements for spanking. Of course, you may not be quiet when it stripes your bare skin, so that will be the difficulty."

She forced herself to breathe.

"Kiss it and thank me for your spanking."

She lowered her lips to the handle, smelling the scent of new leather as she kissed it. "Thank you for spanking me, sir," she said.

He took the wicked-looking loopy johnny away from her and pressed a hand down on her low back.

She waited, her bottom crawling in anticipation of the first stroke.

It came so much worse than she'd expected. The loops bit into her skin, stinging like a thousand wasps.

She pressed her hips forward against the desk as if to get away and clamped her mouth shut on her cry, closing her throat. It was a full three seconds before she could breathe, the pain sending pinpricks of heat everywhere in her body.

He brought it down again and once more she lurched forward, wanting to crawl over the top of the desk and off to the other side. He struck her two more times and she reached back to cover her poor bottom, certain she couldn't take any more.

"Miss Bell, you will remove your hands at once."

"Please," she whispered. "Please, sir."

"The spanking is not over until I decide. I will add three strokes for every second it takes you to—"

She yanked her hands away.

"Thank you." He delivered another searing stroke.

She clamped her lips together, whimpering.

Another terrible stripe. Then another.

"Oh, please," she pleaded with any sense of dignity at all. Hot tears clung to her eyelashes.

Ben pulled up her panties, which chafed horribly, despite the fact that they were made of the softest satin. Lowering her skirt, he turned her around.

His face still held the stern mask, but he drew her into his arms, kissing her hair and rubbing her back.

"Ow," she whimpered as the understatement of the year.

Ben cupped her nape in that possessive way of his, his hard muscled body powerful, even when disguised in a suit. She breathed in his masculine scent, trying to calm the trembling in her body. She felt thoroughly punished by him—a delicious feeling, really, now that she knew he'd forgiven her.

Her legs wobbled beneath her, but Ben held her up with one strong arm around her waist. He nuzzled her ear, then her neck.

"I hate the loopy johnny," she complained into his jacket.

He pulled her head back to look down at her, amusement crinkling his eyes. "I found it quite effective. It will stay here in my office for times when you require my immediate correction."

Moisture leaked onto her panties.

"It might get misplaced. You know, by the cleaners or something."

He caught her chin with his index finger and raised a stern eyebrow. "It had better not disappear or you will not sit for a week, understand?"

Her pussy clenched.

"You're mean," she whispered, lifting her lips up to be kissed by him, her alpha wolf who had taken her so deftly in hand.

BEN WATCHED from the bed as Ashley padded naked from the shower into their bedroom. A growl rose in his throat just watching the bounce of her bare breasts as she walked. When she bent over to search through her underwear drawer, giving him full view of her juicy ass, her sex peeking from between her legs, his skin pricked with heat.

"Come here," he said, pushing himself to sit, his voice deeper than normal.

She erected herself and turned, looking over her shoulder at him. Her hands instantly went to cover her ass, and he chuckled.

"The marks are gone from yesterday; looks like you've left me a blank canvas again," he said.

She looked wary. "You didn't bring that horrible thing home, did you?"

He grinned. "No. But I did purchase a few other implements when I bought the loopy johnny."

She shivered, but her feet moved, bringing her to the bed. "You and I both know you don't need anything but your hand," she said, affecting a pout. "Shifter strength and all."

"Yes, but that would get boring. Five spankings, all with my hand? No. I have to mix it up a little."

He patted his lap and she dutifully folded over it, the scent of her arousal bringing the animal in him to the surface. Despite his threats, he didn't use anything but his palm, making it sting, but keeping the intensity to a medium level. He watched as her skin turned from peaches and cream to pink and then to red. When the color began to hold, he stopped and rubbed.

She wriggled over his legs in an open invitation. He reached for the bedside table, where he'd stored his new toys, and pulled out the bottle of lubricant. Parting her cheeks, he dribbled some on her anus, chuckling when she clenched her cheeks and tried to roll away.

"I think it's time we prepare your ass to take my cock," he said, using an observational tone as he grasped her hips and repositioned her, lifting her bottom and angling it perfectly. He gave her another dozen spanks for good measure.

"No-o," she moaned. "Your cock is way too big. It won't fit."

"First of all, little girl, you will take my cock anywhere I choose to put it. Second, you are being punished, so your pleasure is hardly a concern to me, and third, I have something here to help prepare the way." He pressed the bulbous tip of a butt plug against her puckering hole. "Open for me, Ashley," he commanded.

She continued to squeeze against the intrusion.

He changed hands and delivered several swift spanks to the backs of her thighs.

"Ow," she squealed. "Ow, okay! I'm sorry."

He waited as first her cheeks relaxed, and finally, the tight ring of muscles eased to accept the stainless steel plug. He pressed it forward, going slowly to give her time to get used to the stretch.

"Ohhh, oh," she moaned. "Oh—oooh." Her voice raised in pitch at the end.

"This plug stays in until I take it out, understand?"

She looked over her shoulder. "Do you mean, I have to wear it to work?" she asked with disbelief.

"Yes." He gave her ass a light swat. "Now get dressed."

She blushed as she climbed off his lap with the plug embedded in her ass, the jeweled handle making a delectable sight between her cheeks. Her walk looked stiff as she returned to her underwear drawer and rooted through, occasionally reaching back to touch the plug.

Satisfied, he crawled out of bed and headed for the shower.

They drove to work in a comfortable silence, although he noticed Ashley's face occasionally turned pink, as if she'd suddenly remembered the plug in her ass.

He'd been in his office only an hour before she tapped on his door and came in.

"I know this is punishment, but..." Her forehead crinkled with anxiety.

He crooked his finger at her. "Come here."

She turned to lock the door.

He patted his lap.

She looked around, even though his blinds were closed and the door was locked. Licking her lips, she leaned over and draped herself across his lap.

He stroked her bottom through her skirt, dragging out her time in the humiliating position. Eventually, he slid her skirt up and her panties down. Grasping the plug, he pushed it in and out of her a few times, eliciting a low moan. "This is what I'm going to do to you tonight with my cock," he promised. "After your last spanking."

She moaned again.

He eased the plug from her ass and wrapped it in a tissue. Pulling up her panties, he helped her to her feet. "Get out," he said, returning to the brusque way of communicating that had earned him the nickname 'Stone man' at the corporation.

It disconcerted her, as he'd hoped, and she straightened her skirt, appearing off-balance as she headed for the door.

He looked at his watch. "We'll be leaving early today. Four o'clock. Be ready."

She ducked to hide her smile. "Yes, sir."

AT FOUR O'CLOCK on the dot, Ashley headed for Ben's office door, tapping on it.

He looked up from his desk. "Ready?"

"Yes, sir."

He closed his laptop and picked it up, sliding it into the same briefcase where she had planted a laptop bomb that might have killed him. She still shuddered to think what might have happened if he hadn't sniffed out the plot against him.

They took the elevator to the parking garage and Ben walked her to her side of the car, but instead of opening the door for her, he pushed her against the side of his Mustang, his considerable erection pressing against her low back.

"Little girl, I'm going to eat you up," he growled in her ear.

"I'm not afraid of the big, bad wolf," she murmured, pressing her ass back for him.

"If you're not careful, you're going to get yourself fucked right here in this parking garage, is that what you want?"

Her breath caught and she couldn't answer, the truth too tangled up and confusing to understand. Yes, of course she wanted to be fucked right then and there and the danger of being seen would make it off the charts hot. But no… no way. She definitely couldn't face getting caught like this. "No, sir," she forced herself to say.

He eased off her and reached past to open her door, smirking at her as she sank into the seat.

At home, he told her to wait to get out of the car. Walking around, he opened her car door and pulled her out, tossing her over his shoulder in one swift movement.

"Oomph," she grunted. "What are you doing?"

He slapped her upturned bottom as he carried her into the house.

"Do you remember the first time I spanked you?" he asked, setting her down in their bedroom, where rope had mysteriously appeared on the bed.

She eyed it, wondering what he was up to. "Yes."

"Yes, sir," he corrected.

"Yes, sir."

He wrapped the rope around her wrists, binding them together, then stringing them up over her head, looping them over the bathroom door.

Now she understood. The night she had planted the bomb in his briefcase and first discovered he was a werewolf, he had taken her to a motel and strung her up this way, taking off her skirt and whipping her with a belt.

He stood behind her now, sliding his hands under her blouse to cup her breasts. His fingers found her nipples, and he pinched and twisted them, finding that perfect balance of pain and pleasure that put her over the edge.

Having her arms lifted overhead made her breasts feel all the more vulnerable, and she twisted, trying to protect herself.

He unzipped her skirt and let it fall in a puddle at her feet. Her panties came off next, then he began to unbutton her blouse, still standing behind her. It felt intimate and sensuous to have him undressing her like a child.

She heard the whoosh of his belt sliding out of the loops and goosebumps raised on her arms.

"Spread your legs."

Although he had her strung up almost to her tiptoes, she managed to widen her stance.

"If you move, my belt will catch your hip or thigh and you won't like that. Can you hold still for your spanking, Ashley?"

"Yes, sir," she murmured.

"Good girl."

He wound the belt buckle end around his fist

and let it fly, catching her right across the middle of her buttocks.

She shrieked, her feet leaving the floor, her body skittering to the side, suspended by the ropes over the door.

"What did I say about holding still?"

"Sorry," she gasped, putting her toes out to stop her and scrambling back into position.

He swung the belt again.

Another searing stripe landed across her ass.

This time she managed not to jump away, but just barely.

She drew in a shaky breath and held it.

Another stripe, then another. Each one he laid seemed worse than the one before, and the earliest ones had begun to burn and smart with a delayed onset of pain.

He caught her across the backs of her thighs and she howled in protest, but miraculously managed not to move. Another stroke, then another until her entire bottom was blazing and her breath came in little pants.

"Three more," he announced.

She thought he might go easier on her, but they were the worst yet, stripes laid across stripes, lines of fire that made her bite her lip and tears spring into her eyes.

He dropped the belt and caught her up by the waist, lifting her weight off the floor to free her from the doorway. When he lowered her and turned her around, she leaped at him, wrapping her legs around his waist and putting her bound wrists over his head.

He carried her to the bed and set her down, extricating himself from her stranglehold. "Your punishment is almost over," he said as he unwound the rope from her wrists. He turned her and pushed her torso down so she folded over the edge of the bed.

"From now on, any time I have to punish you for something serious, you will be taking it in the ass afterward."

She shivered, half excited, half terrified. The size of Ben's cock made this punishment all the more daunting, even if she hadn't been an anal sex virgin.

He walked around to the bedside table, where he picked up a tube of lubricant.

"Reach back and hold your cheeks apart for me."

She squeezed her eyes closed, humiliated by the instructions. Her body seemed to love his degradation, though, her pussy leaking arousal onto her thighs as she obeyed. She flinched at the touch of the lubricant, cool and slick against her quivering anus.

Ben unzipped his pants, dropping them to the floor. He never wore boxers or briefs because they only impeded him if he wanted to shift quickly. His manhood stood out now, in its full glory, waving at her ass with intent.

She turned back to face the bed and grasped a fistful of the covers.

He pushed the head of his cock against her most private entrance and held it there, not forcing, but insisting.

She took a deep breath and exhaled, willing herself to relax.

He seized the opportunity and pushed harder, breaching her entrance.

She gasped at the ring of fire as she stretched wide to accommodate him.

He eased in, centimeter by centimeter.

In each moment she was sure she couldn't take more of him, and yet he did not stop, filling her with his huge cock until at last she felt the contact of his hips against her ass.

"Good girl," he crooned and she relaxed, his praise filling her with purpose.

He slid out and back in, and the sensation felt too intense for her to enjoy. Nevertheless, her pussy thrummed with excitement, desperate for touch.

Seeming to know just what she needed, Ben reached around the front of her and slid his fingers over her swollen slit.

She moaned, pressing herself against his fingers, eager for more.

He slowly set a pace, fucking her ass with his enormous cock as his fingers found her clit.

It was far too much—too much pleasure, too much intensity, too much fear of pain. The pain itself had disappeared.

"Ben," she whimpered.

"You're doing so well, *amorcita*. Are you ready to come?"

"Yes… yes, please. Yes, sir," she babbled.

He rubbed her clit harder at the same time he picked up the pace of his fucking, filling her, sending her over the edge with a cry of ecstasy. And yet she found she couldn't climax—or at least not the way she usually did, because when her muscles clenched, her anus tightened around his cock, bringing the pain back.

She relaxed instead, surrendering as he pumped in and out and in again, shoving deep inside her and giving a shout of release. The waves of pleasure following an orgasm flowed through her, so perhaps it had been a climax after all.

He eased out and carried her to the shower, where he held her up and let the water clean them both.

She leaned back against him, her eyes closed, water running down her face. "Am I forgiven?" she asked, already knowing the answer, but wanting to hear it.

Ben wrapped his hand around her neck and

pulled her head back to bite her ear. "Don't ever lie to me again," he growled, sending shivers running up and down her spine.

"I won't," she said, "I promise."

"I love you," he said. "No matter what. Remember that."

Tears warmed her eyes. "How did I get so lucky?"

He kissed her ear. "No," he murmured. "I'm the lucky one."

The End

EXTENDED EXCERPT FROM THE ALPHA'S HUNGER

Ashley picked up her satchel with Ben Stone's laptop and stepped into the elevator. Her limbs dragged, weak from being so wound up for past twenty-four hours.

It's almost over. Then Melissa will be safe and you can go to the police and tell Mr. Stone what you've done.

She took the elevator to the third floor of the parking garage and got off. Clutching the satchel to her chest, she walked forward, toward the northwest corner. She had parked her car there that morning just to familiarize herself with the area. The cement walls echoed with her footsteps, the smell of exhaust and gasoline oppressive. The lot seemed empty—no other cars, no people, nothing. She stood and waited. Had she heard the time or place wrong? No, the words were still echoing in her mind. *Third floor, northwest corner of the lot.* She opened her car door and sat down on the seat with the door standing open. Sweat trickled down her ribs. She thought she heard a door close, but when she looked around, she only saw the stairwell door, and no one was near it.

Time ticked by. Five minutes, then ten.

God, she hoped Melissa was okay.

Suddenly, she heard the sound of a car coming up the ramp. She stood up and took the laptop out of the satchel, her hands clumsy. The satchel dropped to the ground and she left it, craning her neck to get a look at the car.

A dark blue sedan approached. It was old and junky. She didn't know what she'd expected, but it had definitely been something more impressive. A Humvee or something. She took a few steps forward to show herself.

The car stopped and three men got out. She tried to see in the darkened windows for another person. Where was Melissa? The men walked toward her. They were young men—scruffy-looking, with tattooed arms and piercings. They wore t-shirts and jeans and they palmed guns.

"Where's Melissa?" she called out.

"You got the laptop?" one of them asked as they drew closer.

"Maybe," she said, clutching it to her chest and backing toward her car. As if she had any chance of not giving it to them when they were armed and it was three against one. "Where's Melissa?"

"She's in the car. Give us the laptop and you can see her." They had backed her up to her car now, surrounding her.

"I want to see her first."

One of them cocked his gun and held it up to her temple, pushing hard against her skull. "Hand it over," he said as his friend grabbed it and tried to pry it from her chest.

"No," she said struggling.

The guy with the gun smacked her head with it and she fell back against the car. She lost her grip on the laptop and one of them snatched it away.

Another one grabbed her arm and yanked her forward. "You're coming with us, honey," he said.

A terrible snarl sounded from the other side of her car and suddenly a huge black animal leaped over the car, gleaming white teeth snapping. Its jaws closed over the neck of the man holding her and they both tumbled to the ground, the beast snarling and growling as they rolled together. Gunshots rang out from both directions, and the animal yelped and let go, but sprang to its feet, crouching to attack another man. The men continued to fire at the animal, the sound ricocheting around the concrete parking garage. Screaming blared in her ears—her own voice, she realized. The laptop had fallen to the ground and she grabbed it and took off running for their car. If her sister was in it, she needed to get to her.

The animal launched at her, knocking her down. She screamed, expecting it to move in for the kill, but instead it turned, lunging at one of the men.

"Let's go, let's get out of here," one of them yelled, helping up the most severely wounded and dragging him toward their car.

She climbed to her feet to follow, but the wolf—or whatever it was—turned and snarled, blood dripping from its muzzle. She took a step back. It snarled again, blocking her way, then it chased the remaining man, tackling him once, but then taking another gunshot wound that left it lying as the man jumped in the driver's seat and the car screeched off.

She ran a few steps after, then stopped, seeing the beast climb to its feet. She froze. It turned amber eyes on her and growled, low and menacing. It was covered in blood, and its fangs looked razor-sharp. It advanced.

She backed up slowly. "Easy, big guy," she said, her heart in her throat. She didn't make eye contact or any sudden movements. If she could just get to her car, she'd be all right. It continued to follow her, though, his head lowered, fangs bared. The growl was like nothing she'd ever heard before. Unworldly. Terrifying.

EXTENDED EXCERPT FROM THE ALPHA'S HUNGER

Her butt hit the car and she fumbled for the door, not wanting to turn her back on the animal.

The wolf stalked closer and she shrieked, scrambling up on the trunk to get away.

The beast suddenly transformed, growing taller, thinning out. She blinked, thinking she had lost her mind.

Ben Stone stood in front of her, dripping in blood, naked, and looking furious. He yanked open the back door to her car and pulled her off the trunk at the same time. "Get on the floor," he said, pointing to the back seat. "Head down, eyes lowered. *Now*."

Ben slammed the back door on Ashley's huddled form and climbed in the driver seat, where he found her keys on the front seat. He drove like a bat out of hell down to the first floor of the parking garage, stopping behind his car.

He had a hidden button for keyless entry to the trunk, just for occasions like these. He also kept a duffel bag with clothes, spare keys, a wallet with a second set of credit cards, cash and IDs, and other useful items inside. He grabbed the bag and yanked on a pair of jeans.

Pulling out a roll of duct tape, he stalked around to Ashley's car, where she had climbed out.

EXTENDED EXCERPT FROM THE ALPHA'S HUNGER

He grabbed her wrists and wound the tape around them while her eyes rolled around in her head with horror.

Dammit. He had a world of trouble on his hands now. Not only had he allowed his enemies to get away, he'd revealed himself to Ashley, who also belonged on his enemy list.

He caught his breath when he saw her entire side was covered in blood. Shoving her back onto the car seat, he yanked open her blouse. Her skin was blotched with the blood, but he saw no bullet hole or wound.

"Where are you hurt?" he demanded.

"I-I," she swallowed as if her mouth were dry. "I think it's your blood," she croaked.

He exhaled in relief and looked down at his own torso to survey the two gunshot wounds he'd taken. They would heal. He must have bled on her when he tackled her to stop her from going to their car.

He lifted Ashley's ankles and wrapped the duct tape around them, then ripped off a smaller piece for her mouth.

She twisted her head away when he came toward her with it, the whites of her eyes glowing. "Please," she panted, the metallic smell of fear coming off her in waves. "Please don't."

He hesitated.

Don't be soft. She's the enemy.

He pointed a finger in her face. "You make one sound and I'll put you in the trunk. Nod if you understand me."

She bobbed her head up and down.

He slammed the door on her and climbed back in her car, tossing his duffel bag onto the seat beside him. He needed to get out of there before real trouble showed up. Those pathetic boys weren't the brains behind the operation.

He knew Ashley wasn't the mastermind, either, or she wouldn't have been attacked by the men back there. Still, she had sold him out—and that bothered him more than any of the rest of it. Maybe, that first night when he met her, his instincts had gone off because she was a danger to him.

But no, that didn't feel right. It had been attraction, not danger.

He pulled a baseball cap down low over his eyes and took off, out of the parking garage. He got on the highway and drove several miles, weaving in and out of traffic and keeping his eyes glued to his rearview mirror. They didn't seem to have a tail. When he was sure of it, he took the next exit and pulled into a seedy motel on East Colfax—the kind that rented by the hour for cash and no ID.

He opened the back door and grabbed the duct tape again. He taped Ashley's hands to her feet, then wound the tape around the handle of the back seat.

"You make one sound, or you try to escape, and I will kill you. Nod your head if you understand."

She whimpered, panting for breath, but nodded.

"I will be right back. Don't move."

He slammed the door again and checked into a room. When he returned to the car, he cut her feet free and tossed a sweatshirt over her bound hands. "Let's go," he said, hauling her out of the car. "Not one sound out of you."

She looked around wildly, but didn't make a peep other than the sound of her breath rasping in her chest.

He took her into the room and used a length of rope to string her wrists up over the bathroom door. She stood on her tiptoes, swaying. Turning his back on her, he washed up, cleaning his gunshot wounds, which had nearly stopped bleeding. The bullets would come out in a few days. Shifters had incredible healing abilities. He rinsed his mouth out to rid the taste of blood and spit.

He was impressed that Ashley still hadn't made a sound. He'd expected some kind of noise by this point. He turned back to her, considering.

"All right, Ashley. I'm going to ask you some questions and you're going to answer." He fished in his duffel bag for his belt and pulled it out. Walking behind her, he unzipped her skirt and let it fall to the floor.

"Wh-what are you doing?" she asked, sidling as far away from him as her bound wrists would allow.

"Baring my target."

She whimpered, twisting and turning and looking up at the ropes binding her hands.

He ignored her antics and pulled her panties down just below her buttocks. He stood back to admire the view. He wasn't surprised to find her ass as perfect as he'd imagined it. Picking up the belt, he wound the buckle end around his fist.

Her eyes bulged. He caught her hips and turned her to face away from him. "I suggest you hold still," he warned just before he brought his belt down across her buttocks with a light slap to perfect his aim.

She shrieked, dancing away from him, her feet lifting from the floor and kicking in the air. His intention had been to intimidate her, and it seemed to be working, because he knew that hadn't really hurt her. He caught her wrists and pinned them against the door to hold her in place. He struck again, just a little harder.

She jumped as if shocked by electricity, her feet dancing to one side.

"Who hired you to kill me?" he demanded.

Noises came out of her, but they were incoherent sputtering.

He whipped her again. "I asked you a question," he growled. "Who hired you to kill me?"

A string of nonsense syllables erupted from her, tumbling from her mouth one after the next.

He considered. He'd wanted her scared, but having her too terrified to speak wouldn't work. Walking around the front of her, he pulled out his knife. Her eyes rolled back when he lifted the blade. He cut her down just as her eyelids fluttered and she fainted.

Damn.

He caught her limp form as it tumbled down and carried her to the bed where he sat with her cradled in his arms.

Within a few seconds her eyes opened and she blinked, looking up at his face.

He brushed the hair back from her big blue eyes and they looked at each other. Propping her up on his knee, he said, "Okay, we're going to try this again. I need answers from you and you're going to give them to me."

She immediately began to struggle, twisting in his arms as if to dive off his lap. He used it to his advantage, pulling her face down over his knees. Her panties were still tangled around her thighs. His hand slapped down on her bare ass with a satisfying smack. She had a perfect bottom for spanking—plump and round, muscled globes that led into shapely thighs.

He slapped one side, then the other, over and over again. He'd just wanted to make her talk without actually harming her, but as he spanked her, his anger over her betrayal ebbed, turning to sympathy as she kicked and wriggled and her beautiful ass turned rosy and then a darker shade of pink. He held her snugly against his body and took care not to slap too hard. Shifters had superhuman strength, and the idea of bruising or actually harming his little assistant didn't sit well with him. Even if she had tried to kill him.

"How much did you get paid for killing me?"

"I didn't—"

He spanked the back of her thigh, causing her to yelp and kick. "How much?"

"Ow... ah... I wasn't trying to kill you. All I had to do was take your laptop," she gasped in a rush.

"And leave the one with the explosives in it."

She went still for a moment, her head lifting.

His heart skipped a beat. She hadn't known about the bomb. Satisfaction warmed his blood. He rested his hand on her blazing cheeks.

"Who gave you the laptop?"

"I don't know."

He resumed spanking. "Who hired you?"

"No one hired me."

He spanked harder.

"Wait!" she cried. "It's true—no one hired me. They kidnapped my sister!"

He froze, his hand mid-air.

"They said they would bring her tonight, but she wasn't there." Ashley's voice sounded strangled.

Ashley abruptly found herself lifted upright and plopped on Ben's knee, his green eyes boring through her.

"It's true," she whispered, seeing he was searching for something in her face.

"You should have come to me," he said, his voice hard like steel.

Her bottom throbbed, his jeans rough against her bare skin. She swallowed. "They said they'd kill her," she croaked.

He pursed his lips. The intensity with which he regarded her had an animal-like quality—as if he was a hunter and she his prey.

The memory of the huge wolf leaping over her car flashed in her mind. "What are you?" she whispered.

Abruptly, he stood, shoving her to her feet. "Go stand in the corner with your panties down," he said, pointing to the juncture of two walls, his expression dangerous.

She didn't even think of not obeying—he had

her so cowed, she would have dropped to her knees and licked his shoe if he'd ordered it.

She shuffled across the room, putting her nose in the corner, intensely aware of her bare ass on full display. She wondered how red it looked. Her cheeks felt hot and stingy and for some bizarre reason, her pussy pulsed in rhythm with the throb there.

"I'm stepping outside. Don't move, not even an inch from that corner. If you do, I will spank you again and this time it will be with my belt."

She shivered, but need made her dare to ask, "What if I have to pee?" She peeked over her shoulder at him.

His eyes narrowed. "Do you?"

"Yes."

"Go now, then," he said.

She walked toward the bathroom, grabbing one side of her panties with her bound hands and trying to pull them up.

"Leave them," he barked.

She looked over to find him trailing behind her toward the bathroom.

"What are you doing?"

"Keeping an eye on you." He leaned in the doorway to the bathroom and folded his arms across his chest.

She willed herself to stop blushing as she sat on the toilet and stared at a spot on the floor. When she finished, she wrestled with the toilet paper, the duct tape making it hard for her to wipe herself.

"Need some help?" he asked.

Was that the glimmer of a smirk on his lips? She glared at him. "No." She started to pull up her panties, then stopped, figuring he'd bark at her again.

"That's right," he said, motioning her forward. "Panties stay down until I pull them up."

She made a huffing sound and tried to walk without shuffling, back to the corner.

"Stay."

Woof. She didn't say it out loud.

Her boss was a werewolf. A huge, black, terrifying beast who somebody had tried to use her to kill. Why? And what would he do with her now?

She stood holding her breath as he left. Her bottom was on fire, and the humiliating position infuriated her, but she was very well aware of the fact that he hadn't hurt her. Well, other than her backside. Considering she'd just seen him trying to rip throats out with huge, sharp fangs, that said something.

The memory of him standing shirtless over her, tearing open her blouse and examining her with concern flitted before her eyes. Even though he thought she'd tried to kill him, he'd been checking her for injuries. He'd rescued her from those men, who had been trying to take her with them.

EXTENDED EXCERPT FROM THE ALPHA'S HUNGER

The motel door opened and closed and she sensed him behind her.

His thumbs hooked under the elastic of her panties, sending an electric shock where they touched her skin. Despite it all—despite her terror that he was going to kill her, despite the rather sound spanking he'd given her, despite the humiliation he'd just subjected her to, her body thrummed just to be near him.

He slowly drew her panties up, an act that seemed more intimate even than if they'd just had sex. Her pussy clenched.

"Good girl," he murmured, his breath hot in her ear. Her nipples puckered. Shivers of electric excitement ran through her body, but too soon, he stepped back. "Put on your skirt, we're leaving."

"Where are we going?" she asked, her knees weak as she tried to step into her skirt without falling.

"You're not in a position to ask questions," he said and gave her panty-clad bottom another slap.

"Am I your prisoner?"

He pulled the pillowcase off one of the pillows and used it to cover her bound wrists as he led her to the door. "Yeah. You're my prisoner." His voice was deep and gruff and it seemed to enter her body and send shockwaves from her core down her legs.

He led her to her car and opened the back door. "Get in."

She slid into the back seat. He immediately pushed her down to lie on the seat and taped her wrists to the base of the front seat, preventing her from sitting up. He leaned over her with the pillowcase open and she realized his intent.

"Wait, no," she shrieked as the case came down over her head.

The car door slammed.

"Mr. Stone," she cried. "Ben! Please. Please take it off." She struggled to dislodge it, rubbing her head against the seat.

The car started.

"Please. Please," she begged.

"Calm down, Ashley. I can't have you seeing where I'm taking you."

The car began to move.

"Get this off me. Get this fucking thing—" She thrashed around, yanking at her wrists to get them free. "Oh, God," she moaned when it seemed clear he wasn't going to take it off and she couldn't get it off on her own. "Oh, God."

Panic took over. She couldn't breathe. She screamed over and over again, drawing in short gasps of breath between shrieks. Her feet kicked at the door, her bound wrists thrashed so much she punched herself in the face.

The car swerved and braked hard.

Oh, crap, she'd made him mad. He was going

to put her in the trunk. She tried to stop screaming, but she couldn't get control.

The car door opened and the pillowcase came off with a whoosh. He reached for her and she cowered, thinking he would strike her. Instead his large hands grasped her head, cupping it, stilling her. His palms were over her ears, muffling her sense of sound. The forced quiet gave her a strange sense of security, as if she was cocooned safely by those hands, protected.

He was leaning over her, his brows drawn together with the same expression he'd worn when he thought she'd been hurt. Pained—like her panic attack had caused him pain. And he'd shrugged off his own bullet wounds. Which… what the hell had happened to them? He wasn't even bleeding anymore, nor did she see any sign of a bandage under his tight-fitting t-shirt.

"You're claustrophobic." It was a statement, rather than a question.

She nodded rapidly, still unable to catch her breath.

He began to fold the pillowcase lengthwise. She jerked away when he held it up to her head, but he persisted, wrapping it over her eyes like a blindfold. It wasn't long enough for him to tie in the back, though.

"I won't look. I'll lie down and I won't look, I promise," she promised, still shaking like a leaf.

He ignored her, pulling out the duct tape. Once more, he positioned the pillowcase over her eyes, then wrapped the duct tape all the way around her head, securing the fabric like a crown around her head. "There," he said. "Lie down."

A wedge of fresh fear shot up and she groped wildly for him, her fingers landing on his t-shirt, which she wrapped up in her fist. His heavy hand dropped onto her nape. He muttered a curse, then pulled her out of the car.

She panicked, twisting wildly in his grip. "Not the trunk. Please—not the trunk. I'll be good, I promise."

To her shock, he wrapped his arms around her and held her against his chest. He didn't say a word, but there was no mistaking the intended comfort. She clung to him, her body trembling against his hard muscled form. She drank in his strength, the solidity of his body. Inch by inch, her body relaxed.

"You're not going in the trunk," he said gruffly. "You're riding up front with me."

"Oh." She willed herself to stop shaking as she took a deep breath. He released her from the embrace and wrapped a firm arm around her waist, guiding her forward and around the car. He followed her head in with his hand as she sat, the way the cops do on crime shows. His weight pressed against her and she heard the click of her seatbelt.

Returning to the driver side, he climbed in. She

heard the rustle of movement, then he grasped her head and pulled her down until it connected with his thigh. He'd put something soft over the center console—a sweatshirt, maybe. She appreciated the thoughtfulness. "Stay down," he said, a note of warning in his voice.

She brought her bound wrists to his leg and wrapped her hands around it, as if he were her security blanket, and she just needed to feel his warmth to stay calm.

He put the car in gear and backed out, one hand still on her nape holding her down. Except then his hand began to move. His fingers threaded into her hair and closed into a fist, tugging slightly but not hurting her. They opened and closed again.

She held perfectly still, not wanting him to stop. She imagined his hands gripping other parts of her body, his touch rough, his grasp firm. What would it be like to be taken by him? Did werewolves have sex with humans? The image of him rolling with his opponent in wolf form, all snarls and teeth, returned to her.

What was he going to do with her? Maybe it was Stockholm syndrome, but she wanted to believe he would take care of her. That he wouldn't harm her.

But what about Melissa? She was someone's prisoner right now, too—if she was still alive. Had she been harmed? How had her captors treated her?

Ashley needed to escape Ben Stone and get to her sister with the laptop before it was too late. She needed to get her head back in the game and come up with a plan, right away.

Ben didn't mean to make love to Ashley's hair with his hand, but once he'd buried his fingers in the glossy, thick mane, it became a compulsion. He stroked along the back of her head, twisting it up into fistfuls and releasing it. Damn, he wanted her.

He'd smelled her arousal when he'd put her in the corner. It had shocked him. He'd just scared her to the point of fainting and then spanked her until her ass turned rosy and she still wanted him? His cock stiffened at the thought. What about this human woman affected him so strongly?

She shifted her position, pulling her hands away from his leg and moving her feet. She was probably completely cramped in the position in which he'd put her. Her foot tangled with her purse where he'd thrown it on the passenger side floor.

It took him a moment to realize she was stealthily moving the bag closer to her. He watched, waiting to see what she was up to. She made another shuffling movement and used it to shove the bag up underneath her hands.

Bile rose in his throat, the wound from her earlier deception still raw. He willed his breathing to stay in control as she rolled her body forward, her face pressing into his leg. Her bound hands dropped into the bag, as if idly hanging there. When they emerged, she clutched her phone.

He pulled the car over to the side and threw it in park. In a swift motion, he hauled her torso further over his lap and whipped up her skirt.

"What do you think you're doing?" he demanded, snatching the phone from her hand. Yanking her panties into her crack, he landed several hard spanks on her sit spots with it. It was a stretch to reach her backside in the awkward position, but he managed it, punishing her already red bottom while she writhed and squirmed beneath him. She had a wide, thin phone and its plastic case made a satisfying thwap each time it connected with her rosy flesh. "Dammit, Ashley! Was the claustrophobia just a big ruse? Were you just tricking me to earn my sympathy?"

"No," she shrieked. "No, it wasn't a trick. Stop, please. Ouch!"

"I will stop when I have made my disgruntlement clear."

She wriggled over his lap as he continued to

spank her. "Ow, stop!" She sank her teeth into his left thigh.

Rather than anger him, it had the odd effect of making him want to throw her down and fuck her brains out. Female wolves bite and snarl while having sex, and she had just flipped a switch in him. His vision domed and his teeth sharpened with the need to mark her. He leaned his head back against the seat, closing his eyes and breathing deeply to regain control.

She didn't take the pause in spanking as a victory, huddled tense and still on his lap. "I'm sorry," she said in a small voice.

He didn't open his eyes. "Who were you going to call?" he asked in a tired voice.

"No one. I just need my phone… in case they call."

Irritation cut through his arousal, bringing him back to his rational self. "Did you think I wouldn't let you answer it? Setting up a new meeting is key to me figuring out who the hell is behind this."

Her little hands pawed at his jeans, plucking the fabric. "Sorry," she said in a small voice. "I didn't know." After a moment of silence, she said, "I was thinking I might text them."

"Blindfolded?"

"Well, getting the blindfold off was my next problem."

He made a growling sound. "What were you going to text?"

"Something like, *I still have the laptop and I want my sister.*"

He handed her the phone and pulled up the blindfold by an inch. "Go ahead."

She texted the words and showed him first before hitting send. He took the phone from her and put it in his pocket, then pushed the blindfold back in place. "You don't move without my permission, understand?"

"Yes, sir."

He sighed and started the car back up.

"What about my sister?"

"We'll find her," he said.

She pushed herself up, her elbow going into his erection.

"Ouch." He jerked and pulled her back down to the original position. "Stay."

"Woof."

He almost smiled at that. Damn, she really tweaked him. He let himself touch her hair again, telling himself it was only to move it out of her face. But that didn't make sense, since she couldn't see anyway. The silky strands slid between his fingers as he pulled back on the road and tried to ignore the sight of her ass, still on display and flossed with her panties. The smell of her arousal filled the car like aromatherapy for his already raging libido.

He pulled up at the old warehouse his brother's pack used as a meeting place. No other cars were there, but that didn't mean anything. Mark Ruhl had talked him through disarming the explosives on the phone, but he'd arranged to meet him here to give him the laptop so he could analyze it, and monitor when the signal was sent for it to detonate. While at the motel, he'd called Stanley and asked him to come to the meeting as well. He would need a ride back to Stone Tech to get his car and the laptop and he needed someone to watch Ashley while he went. It wouldn't be safe to bring her back to the scene.

He entered cautiously, scenting the air. Empty. He pulled off the pillowcase blindfold once they were inside. Pointing to an old couch against one wall, he said, "Sit."

She glared at him, but obeyed.

"Little girl," he said, "You need to stop giving me those dirty looks, or I will take you back over my knee for a reminder of who is in charge around here."

She wobbled on her feet, and he would swear the look she gave him was pure desire, but she looked hastily away.

"That's better," he said, his voice thicker than usual.

He lifted his head, catching a sound at the back door. It pushed open and Stanley and three other males strode in, naked. Shifters were unabashed about nudity, but for the first time, he found himself bothered, not liking the way Ashley stared at them. They grabbed clothes from their lockers, stalking over, eyeing her. He became acutely aware of how out of place she looked, still dressed in her narrow work skirt and heels, her blood-stained blouse gaping because he'd popped all the buttons off when he tore it open to check for injury. Why the hell hadn't he put her in his shirt first?

"Hey, Stanley," he said. "Hey, guys."

"Who's she?"

"You don't need to know," he said. To Ashley, he said, "Lower your eyes."

She obeyed him, although he could see she was alert and paying attention.

"You brought a human to our private location," Stanley stated the obvious, his eyes narrowed.

"She was blindfolded."

"She knows what we are." He folded his arms across his chest.

"I'll handle her."

"How?"

The general code was to kill outsiders who found out. He bristled. "It's my problem and I'll take care of it."

Stanley raised his brows, looking at Ashley dubiously. "She looks like trouble."

WANT MORE? ALPHA'S PROMISE

When one Alpha makes a promise to another, his word is bond.

Still, when Cody promises the Denver pack alpha he'll rescue his sister-in-law from danger, he doesn't account for the mayhem the tightly-wound human female will bring to his life. He has no idea how to survive with her under his roof when he finds her scent so incredibly delectable. When he craves her lush body more than his next breath.

But the sexy real estate agent is too prim and polished for his rough style, too ungrateful for his help, and way too apt to get herself back into trouble.

What she may need is a bit of his wolf-style discipline…

WANT MORE? ALPHA'S PROMISE

Publisher's Note: This book was originally published by Stormy Night Publications in 2016. The author has made a few alterations to the original text. The book includes spankings and rough, intense sexual scenes. If such material offends you, please don't buy this book.

READ NOW —> http://mybook.to/alphaspromise

WANT FREE RENEE ROSE BOOKS?

Go to http://subscribepage.com/alphastemp to sign up for Renee Rose's newsletter and receive a free copy of *Alpha's Tempta-*

tion, Theirs to Protect, Owned by the Marine, Theirs to Punish, The Alpha's Punishment, Disobedience at the Dressmaker's and *Her Billionaire Boss.* In addition to the free stories, you will also get special pricing, exclusive previews and news of new releases.

OTHER TITLES BY RENEE ROSE

Paranormal

Wolf Ridge High Series

Alpha Bully

Alpha Knight

Step Alpha

Alpha King

Bad Boy Alphas Series

Alpha's Temptation

Alpha's Danger

Alpha's Prize

Alpha's Challenge

Alpha's Obsession

Alpha's Desire

Alpha's War

Alpha's Mission

Alpha's Bane

Alpha's Secret

Alpha's Prey

Alpha's Sun

Shifter Ops

Alpha's Moon

Alpha's Vow

Alpha's Revenge

Alpha's Fire

Alpha's Rescue

Alpha's Command

Werewolves of Wall Street

Big Bad Boss: Midnight

Big Bad Boss: Moon Mad

Alpha Doms Series

The Alpha's Hunger

The Alpha's Promise

The Alpha's Punishment

The Alpha's Protection (Dirty Daddies)

Two Marks Series

Untamed

Tempted

Desired

Enticed

Wolf Ranch Series

Rough

Wild

Feral

Savage

Fierce

Ruthless

Contemporary

Chicago Sin

Den of Sins

Rooted in Sin

Made Men Series

Don't Tease Me

Don't Tempt Me

Don't Make Me

Chicago Bratva

"Prelude" in Black Light: Roulette War

The Director

The Fixer

"Owned" in Black Light: Roulette Rematch

The Enforcer

The Soldier

The Hacker

The Bookie

The Cleaner

The Player

The Gatekeeper

Alpha Mountain

Hero

Rebel

Warrior

Vegas Underground Mafia Romance

King of Diamonds

Mafia Daddy

Jack of Spades

Ace of Hearts

Joker's Wild

His Queen of Clubs

Dead Man's Hand

Wild Card

Daddy Rules Series

Fire Daddy

Hollywood Daddy

Stepbrother Daddy

Master Me Series

Her Royal Master

Her Russian Master

Her Marine Master

Yes, Doctor

Double Doms Series

Theirs to Punish

Theirs to Protect

Holiday Feel-Good

Scoring with Santa

Saved

Other Contemporary

Black Light: Valentine Roulette

Black Light: Roulette Redux

Black Light: Celebrity Roulette

Black Light: Roulette War

Black Light: Roulette Rematch

Punishing Portia (written as Darling Adams)

The Professor's Girl

Safe in his Arms

Sci-Fi

Zandian Masters Series

His Human Slave

His Human Prisoner

Training His Human

His Human Rebel

His Human Vessel

His Mate and Master

Zandian Pet

Their Zandian Mate

His Human Possession

Zandian Brides

Night of the Zandians

Bought by the Zandians

Mastered by the Zandians

Zandian Lights

Kept by the Zandian

Claimed by the Zandian

Stolen by the Zandian

Rescued by the Zandian

Other Sci-Fi

The Hand of Vengeance

Her Alien Masters

ABOUT RENEE ROSE

USA TODAY BESTSELLING AUTHOR RENEE ROSE loves a dominant, dirty-talking alpha hero! She's sold over two million copies of steamy romance with varying levels of kink. Her books have been featured in USA Today's *Happily Ever After* and *Popsugar*. Named Eroticon USA's Next Top Erotic Author in 2013, she has also won *Spunky and Sassy's* Favorite Sci-Fi and Anthology author, *The Romance Reviews* Best Historical Romance, and has hit the *USA Today* list fifteen times with her Bad Boy Alphas, Chicago Bratva, and Wolf Ranch series.

Renee loves to connect with readers!
www.reneeroseromance.com
reneeroseauthor@gmail.com

facebook.com/reneeroseromance
instagram.com/reneeroseromance
bookbub.com/authors/renee-rose

Made in the USA
Coppell, TX
26 May 2025